The Social Mind

Understanding Vygotsky's Theory of Cognitive Development

Freudian Trips

Copyright Page

Disclaimer

The views and opinions expressed in this book are those of the author(s) and do not necessarily reflect the official policy or position of any other agency, organization, employer, or company. The contents of this book are for informational and educational purposes only and are not intended to serve as professional advice, diagnosis, or treatment.

The information provided in this book is believed to be accurate and reliable as of the date of publication. However, it may include some errors or inaccuracies, and no warranty or guarantee is provided regarding the accuracy, timeliness, or applicability of the content.

Readers are encouraged to consult with professional philosophers, educators, or other qualified professionals where appropriate for personalized advice. The author(s) and publisher shall not be liable for any loss, damage, or harm caused or alleged to be caused, directly or indirectly, by the information or ideas contained, suggested, or referenced in this book.

By reading this book, the reader acknowledges and agrees that they are solely responsible for how they interpret and apply the information contained herein.

This book may also include references to other works, studies, and sources. These references are provided for further reading and exploration and do not imply endorsement or validation of the specific theories, viewpoints, or interpretations presented in those works.

Introduction: The Power of Connection

Imagine learning to ride a bike all by yourself. No one to hold the handlebars as you find your balance, no encouraging words, and no helping hand to pick you up when you fall. It sounds almost impossible, doesn't it? That's because learning, for most of us, isn't a solo act.

For years, many experts studying how children learn focused mainly on what happened inside a child's head – their individual thinking process. But a psychologist named Lev Vygotsky looked at the bigger picture. He believed that to understand how children's minds grow, we can't ignore the world they live in. He saw learning as a social adventure!

Learning Hand-in-Hand

Vygotsky noticed that children don't just learn by exploring on their own. They learn by talking, playing, and interacting with parents, teachers, friends, and their whole community. These interactions give them much more than just information. Adults and older kids help children make sense of things, show them new skills, and encourage them when it gets difficult. It's like they're building a mental bridge together.

Vygotsky believed that our minds are shaped by the people around us and the special traditions, beliefs, and ways of doing things that make up our culture. Let's think about how powerful that is – we don't just inherit our eye color or hair type; we also inherit all this rich knowledge and experience from those around us!

The Social Mind

Vygotsky's ideas turned the way we think about learning on its head. His theory is known as the Sociocultural Theory. That's a fancy way of saying that our minds grow their strongest when they're connected to the world around them. Children aren't just little scientists experimenting by themselves – they're part of a team!

This book will take you on a journey to explore how children's minds develop, not in isolation, but as part of a wonderful, supportive learning community. It's a journey that shows us the incredible power of social interaction in shaping who we become.

Chapter 1: The World Shapes Our Minds

Imagine This...

Think about all the different ways we count things. Here in the United States, we count to ten and then go on to eleven, twelve, and so on. But in some parts of the world, counting systems are based on body parts, where people might use their fingers, toes, and even joints! Different, isn't it?

Differences like this might seem small, but they show us something really important: where you grow up shapes the way you think. This is the starting point of Vygotsky's Sociocultural Theory.

Culture: It's More Than Just Festivals

Culture is the big bubble we all live in. It's the shared ideas, traditions, and tools of our community. Think of things like:

- **The Rules:** How we say hello, how we wait in line, what's right and wrong.

- **The Tools:** Not just hammers and saws! Books, calendars, even the numbers we use are cultural tools.
- **The Stories:** The history and tales that every group shares, passed down from generation to generation.

All of these things are like ingredients in a mental recipe. We don't even realize it, but growing up in our culture shapes the way we solve problems, see the world, and even experience feelings.

Language: The Superpower of the Mind

Vygotsky believed language is one of our culture's most powerful tools. It's more than just words! Think about these ways we use language:

- **Sharing Knowledge:** We explain things, give directions, and even tell amazing stories.
- **Remembering the Past:** Language helps us store information and learn from history.
- **The Inner Voice:** See that little voice in your head? That's for planning, problem-solving, and even controlling emotions!

From the Outside... In

Here's where things get really interesting! Vygotsky believed that we begin learning on the outside, with other people. Picture a toddler learning new words from their mom, or a student getting help with math problems from a friend. This outside knowledge slowly becomes inside knowledge.

This process is called internalization. It's like downloading awesome upgrades for your brain! Every conversation, every story we hear, every time someone teaches us a new skill, it makes our minds a bit stronger and more capable.

The Takeaway

This chapter highlights how culture and communication aren't just around us—they literally build our minds. It shows why Vygotsky was such a game-changer; he made us see that learning isn't just about what's in your own head, but about the incredible power of the world around you.

Chapter 2: Your Learning Dream Team

Remember when you learned to ride a bike? Maybe you had your mom or dad jogging beside you, holding the bike steady until you were ready to try on your own. Or, maybe an older sibling gave you tips and helped you avoid a few wobbles. That's the idea behind something Vygotsky called the "More Knowledgeable Other," or MKO for short.

So, What's an MKO?

An MKO is anyone who knows a bit more or can do something a bit better than you. Think of them like your personal learning coaches:

- **The Obvious Coaches:** Parents, teachers, and experts – the kind of people we usually think of as helping us learn.
- **Star Teammates:** Older siblings, classmates who get a topic faster, even that tech-savvy cousin you can ask for help!

The best part? MKOs can be anyone who lends a helping hand along the way!

Scaffolding: Your Personalized Boost

MKOs don't just throw information at you and wish you luck. They provide something called "scaffolding." Imagine building a super tall tower – a scaffold is the support that helps you build higher and higher.

Here's what scaffolding looks like in learning:

- **Starting Simple:** Breaking down big tasks into small steps you can handle.
- **Extra Support at First:** An MKO might guide you a lot at the beginning, explaining and demonstrating.
- **Fading Away:** As you get the hang of it, they step back, letting you do more yourself.
- **The Perfect Challenge:** It's all about finding the sweet spot between too easy and way too hard!

MKOs in Action

Let's see MKOs in the wild:

- **Baby Talk:** Parents use silly voices, repeat words, and have super simple conversations. All this builds early language skills!
- **Guided Learning:** Teachers don't just lecture at the front of the class. They ask questions, work in small groups, helping students when they get stuck.

- **Playtime Power:** Older siblings help younger ones with toys, games, and even getting dressed. Learning through play is awesome!

The Big Idea

MKOs are like bridges to new knowledge. They tailor their help, figuring out exactly what you need at that moment to reach the next level. It shows that learning's not some lonely struggle; it's about working together to bring out your best!

Chapter 3: The Sweet Spot – Finding Your Zone

Think of learning like climbing a ladder. There are some rungs you can reach all by yourself, some that feel way too high, and then those that are just out of reach... but with a little boost, you could totally get there! This is the heart of Vygotsky's Zone of Proximal Development, or ZPD for short.

Decoding the ZPD

Let's break it down:

- **Zone 1: "I got this!"** These are the skills you've already mastered. You can do these things easily and independently.
- **Zone 2: The "Sweet Spot!"** This is where the magic happens – things you *can't quite* do alone, but with help from an MKO (remember those learning coaches from Chapter 2?), you can learn it!
- **Zone 3: "Whoa, too much!"** These are things way beyond your current abilities, even with help. It's like trying to skip five rungs on the ladder!

The Power of Potential

The ZPD is all about believing in what you can become, not just what you can do right now. It's about pushing your limits just a little bit further each time you learn. Imagine that feeling of finally figuring something out – that's the ZPD at work!

ZPD Spotters: Teachers and Parents

Teachers and parents are like ZPD detectives! They know how to figure out where you are on that learning ladder and what kind of help gets you to the next rung. They might:

- **Ask questions:** To see what you already know and what gets you a bit stumped.
- **Give small hints:** Not the whole answer, just enough to get those brain gears turning.
- **Work together:** Instead of doing it *for* you, they do it *with* you, then slowly back off as you get the idea.

Why the ZPD Rocks

Here's why this zone is so important:

1. **No Boredom:** Learning tasks that are too easy get old fast. The ZPD keeps things interesting!
2. **Less Frustration:** Trying to do stuff that's way too hard leads to feeling discouraged. The ZPD is about the right kind of challenge.
3. **Growth Spurt:** The ZPD is where your brain stretches and grows the most!

The Takeaway

The Zone of Proximal Development shows us that learning is a journey. It's about finding the tasks that are just right – the ones that make you think hard but also give you that amazing "aha!" moment when you nail it. Remember, it's with the help of others that we truly reach our potential!

Chapter 4: Vygotsky's Classroom Makeover

Imagine walking into a classroom buzzing with activity. Kids are working together in small groups, helping each other with experiments, and excitedly discussing a story. The teacher moves around, not lecturing at the front, but listening in on groups, giving a little nudge here and a helpful suggestion there. This is what Vygotsky's ideas look like in action!

Teamwork Makes the Dream Work: Collaborative Learning

Vygotsky believed that learning together is way more powerful than everyone sitting alone. Here's how this works:

- **Mixed-Ability Groups:** Kids at different skill levels team up. Everyone gets a chance to learn and teach!
- **Sharing the Spotlight:** Students explain stuff to each other, which helps them understand even better.
- **Problem-Solving Partners:** Instead of solo struggles, kids tackle challenges together, sharing ideas and building on each other's thinking.

Benefits Bonanza: Kids who learn in teams develop better problem-solving and communication skills. They become more confident and even learn to value different perspectives!

Taking Turns with Reciprocal Teaching

Think of this like a game of learning tag! In reciprocal teaching, students take turns being the "teacher" for small groups. They do things like:

- **Summarizing:** Breaking down the main points of a chapter for their classmates.
- **Question Master:** Asking questions to check if everyone's understanding the material.
- **The Predictor:** Making guesses about what happens next in a story or a science experiment.

This strategy works because it forces everyone to think deeply. The "student-teacher" has to really know the stuff, and the listeners have to be engaged and ask thoughtful questions!

Teachers: The Ultimate Guides

The teacher's role in a Vygotsky-inspired classroom shifts a bit. They're less like a talking textbook and more like an awesome coach:

- **Setting the Stage:** They create interesting projects and activities designed for group learning.
- **Matchmaker:** Carefully placing kids into groups to get the best mix of abilities.

- **Support System:** Offering just enough help - a question, a hint, encouragement - to keep everyone in their ZPD.

Tech Tools: Boosting Vygotsky

Technology can take Vygotsky's ideas to the next level! Here's how:

- **Online Collaboration:** Tools let kids work on projects together, even from outside the classroom.
- **Expert Access:** Students can video chat with scientists, authors, or experts anywhere in the world. Real-world MKOs!
- **Creative Expression:** Tech tools help kids visualize concepts, create presentations, and share ideas in fun new ways.

The Takeaway

Vygotsky's classroom is all about the power of community. It's a place where kids support each other, learn from each other, and celebrate progress together. Teachers become expert guides, giving students the tools and encouragement to reach their full potential. Talk about a learning revolution!

Chapter 5: Vygotsky in Your World

Think Vygotsky's ideas only work inside a classroom? Think again! His focus on learning from others and reaching our potential can be applied just about anywhere – from the home to the office, and even to supporting students with unique needs.

Supercharging Parenting: Vygotsky at Home

Parents are a child's first and most important MKOs. Here's how to put Vygotsky into practice at home:

- **The Power of Play:** Play isn't just about having fun; it's a child's learning laboratory! Playing together lets you guide their thinking and build new skills.
- **Talk It Out:** Simple conversations help tremendously. Explain what you're doing, ask questions to spark their curiosity, and build their vocabulary.
- **Zone Spotter:** Pay attention to what your child can do easily, what they need help with, and what's too difficult. This sweet spot is their ZPD!

- **Celebrate Every Win:** Effort matters! Praising steps forward, even small ones, shows them you believe in their ability to grow.

Leveling Up at Work: Vygotsky in the Office

Who says learning stops when you become an adult? Vygotsky's ideas are great for workplace training, too:

- **Mentorship Matters:** Pairing new employees with experienced ones is like a built-in MKO system on the job!
- **Scaffolding Skills:** Break down complex tasks into smaller steps and provide guidance that fades as the employee becomes more confident.
- **Group Power:** Team projects let people learn from each other and build on each other's strengths.

Inclusive Education: Everyone in the Zone

Vygotsky believed every child has the potential to learn and grow. This is especially important for students with learning differences:

- **No One Left Out:** Classrooms that encourage cooperation and valuing everyone's strengths create a powerful learning community.
- **Tailored Support:** Understanding a student's individual ZPD makes sure they get the right kind of help at the right time.
- **Focus on Potential:** Helping students see their strengths and what they *can* do leads to greater determination and success.

The Big Takeaway

Vygotsky's ideas give us a powerful lens for seeing the world. They remind us that we are never truly alone, whether we are learning, working, or simply trying to figure things out. It's about finding the right support, believing in our potential, and celebrating every step on the journey of becoming the best version of ourselves.

Chapter 6: The Big Discussion – Putting Vygotsky to the Test

Vygotsky's ideas were revolutionary, changing the way we understand learning. But like any big theory, people haven't always agreed on every single point. This chapter is about taking a balanced look and exploring how his ideas have held up over time.

Where Could He Have Done More?

Even brilliant thinkers can't cover everything! Here are some areas where people think Vygotsky's theory could have gone deeper:

- **The Individual Thinker:** Did Vygotsky focus so much on social learning that he underestimated what kids can figure out on their own?
- **Culture's Toolkit:** Vygotsky was right about culture's importance, but could he have said more about how different cultures approach learning in different ways?
- **The Power of Emotions:** Vygotsky talked about how we learn from others, but how much do feelings like

confidence, frustration, or excitement impact learning too?

A Meeting of Minds: Vygotsky and Other Great Thinkers

Vygotsky wasn't the only one with big ideas about how kids develop! Let's see how his work compares to others:

- **Piaget vs. Vygotsky:** Piaget thought kids develop in set stages mostly on their own. Vygotsky focused on the social environment and how it pushes learning forward at any age.
- **Social Constructivism:** This idea says we build knowledge together, not just receive it. This fits perfectly with Vygotsky's view on learning as a team effort!

Vygotsky Gets an Update – Modern Research

Science never stands still! Researchers today continue to build on and test Vygotsky's theories:

- **The Brain Connection:** Brain scans help us see how social interaction actually changes how our brains develop and learn!
- **Tech Tools 2.0:** Are things like video games, simulations, and online learning spaces the modern version of Vygotsky's cultural tools?
- **Global Learners:** Researchers study how Vygotsky's ideas translate across different cultures, making sure they work for everyone.

The Takeaway

The fact that we're still asking questions about Vygotsky's work proves how powerful his ideas remain! A great theory sparks debate and makes us think more deeply. Vygotsky reminded us of the incredible impact of community and support on our minds, and researchers will continue exploring these connections for a long time to come.

Conclusion: The Ripple Effects of Vygotsky

Our journey through Vygotsky's world of learning has shown us that our minds are truly shaped by the people and the culture around us. It may sound simple, but this idea changed everything!

Vygotsky's Greatest Hits: A Quick Review

Let's recap some of his most important contributions:

- **The Social Mind:** Learning isn't just a solo mission; it's powered by connection and cooperation.
- **MKOs: Our Learning Coaches:** Parents, teachers, and anyone who knows a little more can be a guide on our learning path.
- **ZPD: The Challenge Sweet Spot:** Finding tasks that are just a bit beyond what we can do alone fosters amazing growth.
- **Culture's Toolkit:** The unique traditions and ideas of our community shape our very way of thinking.

Classrooms and Beyond: Where Vygotsky Lives On

Vygotsky's ideas have had a tremendous impact on the world:

- **Schools Transformed:** Collaborative learning, group projects, and teachers being guides are all Vygotsky-inspired.
- **Parenting Power:** Parents understand the importance of play, everyday conversations, and supporting development every step of the way.
- **Workplaces That Work:** Training programs focused on mentorship and skill-building use Vygotsky's principles.
- **No Learner Left Behind:** His emphasis on potential benefits all students, especially those with learning challenges.

The Future is Bright: Where Vygotsky's Ideas Can Take Us

Vygotsky's work is far from finished inspiring us! Think about these exciting possibilities:

- **Tech That Teaches:** Can artificial intelligence and virtual reality create amazing new MKOs and learning experiences?
- **Global Connections:** How can we use technology to help students learn from each other and share knowledge across cultures?
- **Unlocking Potential:** Can we understand even better how to tailor support to each individual's ZPD, maximizing everyone's ability to learn?

The Takeaway

Vygotsky taught us that humans are, at our core, social learners. We need each other, we build upon each other's ideas, and we celebrate each other's progress. His theories remind us that learning is an adventure best shared – and that our greatest potential is often found with the help of others.

About Freudian Trips

Welcome to Freudian Trips, your dedicated platform for diving deep into the world of psychology. We are more than just a YouTube channel or a book publisher. We are a beacon of enlightenment, making complex psychological concepts accessible and engaging for all.

Our YouTube channel is a rich repository of psychology made simple. We take the profound and often complex ideas from the world of psychology and break them down into digestible, easy-to-understand content. From the foundational theories of Freud to the cognitive insights of Piaget, we cover a broad spectrum of psychological schools and thoughts, making psychology accessible to everyone, regardless of their background or prior knowledge.

As a book publisher, we take the same approach, transforming intricate psychological theories into comprehensible narratives. Our books are not just collections of words, but vessels of wisdom that make psychology approachable and relatable. We believe that psychology should not be confined to academic circles, but should be available to all who seek to understand the human mind and behavior.

At Freudian Trips, we believe in the power of curiosity and the pursuit of knowledge. We are here to stoke the fires of your curiosity, to guide you on your intellectual journey, and to help you navigate the fascinating world of psychology.

If you are someone who is not afraid to question, to explore, and to learn, then you are in the right place. Join us on this journey of exploration, as we make psychology easy to understand, one concept at a time.

Be sure to visit our Youtube channel at:
www.freudiantrips.com/youtube

You can also visit us on the web at www.freudiantrips.com

Welcome to The Freudian Trip community. Stay curious. Stay enlightened.